The Story of
ZEPHYR WRIGHT

HERO OF THE CIVIL RIGHTS ERA

For Josh
my freedom fighter

When she was born, her mama named her for the wind. Her mama thought, 'the wind can't be stopped, it goes where it pleases.'

Zephyr grew up. She grew strong and smart. Her strong wind wanted to go to college.

Except Zephyr lived in Texas a long time ago, when people knew how to build walls, and doors with locks to keep the wind out.

So only some colleges would let the Zephyr wind in. But when that wind got in it swept up all the learning there was.

Zephyr learned the most about two things: freedom and cooking.

One woman, named 'Lady Bird' liked it so much she unlocked her door and let the Zephyr wind in. Lady Bird wanted Zephyr to cook for her family.

Zephyr was nervous to work behind a locked door. She knew behind this locked door was Lady Bird's husband. He was tall, loud and bossy.

He worked in the government and supported the wall builders and door lockers. Zephyr was nervous but not scared, she knew the wind could go around and even blow over tall, loud and bossy.

Behind this locked door, the Zephyr wind blew up the most delicious food, Lady Bird and all her friends were amazed.

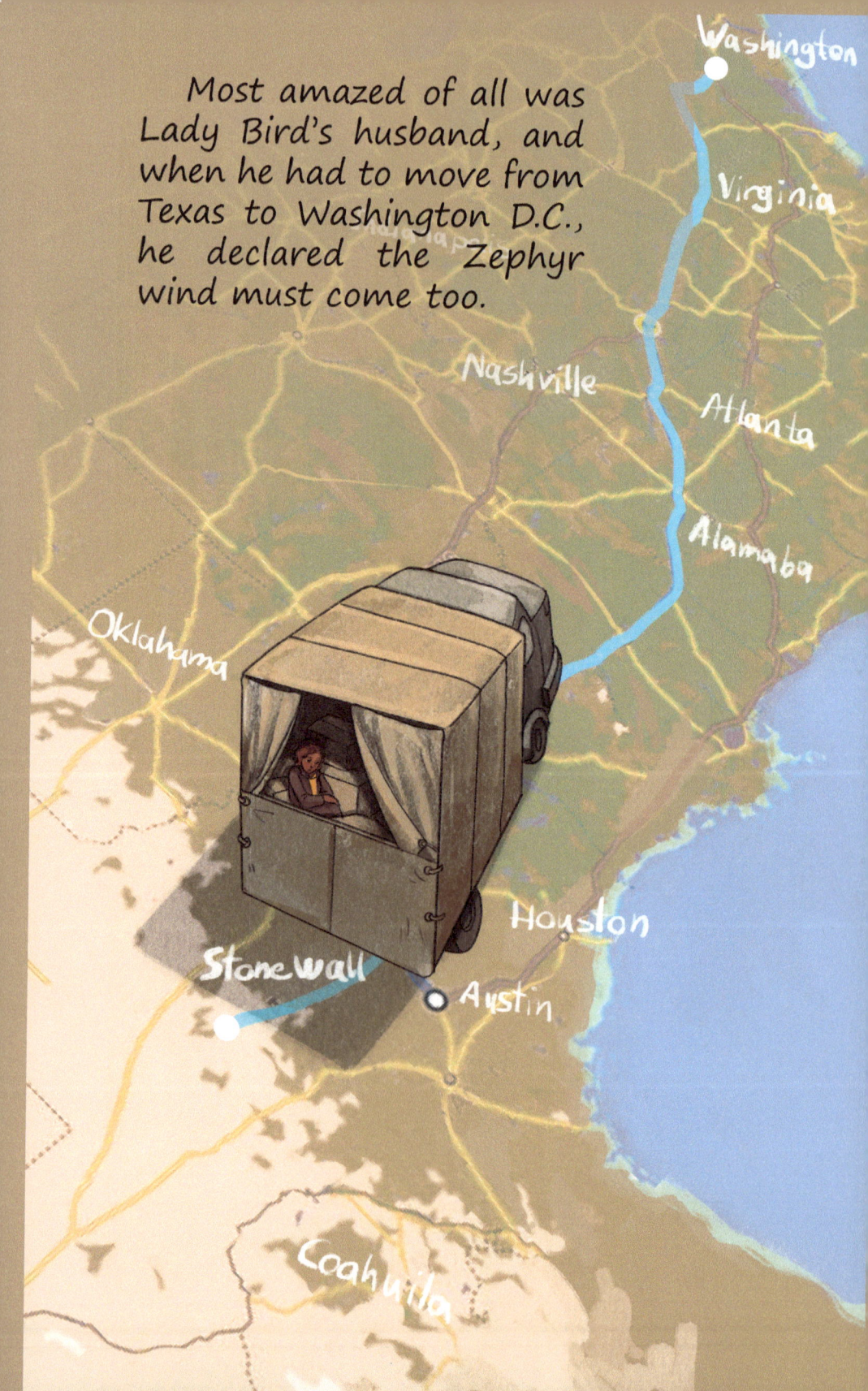

Most amazed of all was Lady Bird's husband, and when he had to move from Texas to Washington D.C., he declared the Zephyr wind must come too.

So Zephyr moved to Washington D.C. But, sometimes Lady Bird needed to go back to Texas. Lady Bird's husband bossed that Zephyr would go too.

The next time Lady Bird's husband bossed Zephyr to go, she said no, she would not. He was angry, but the Zephyr wind blew his loud shouts away.

When he was quiet Zephyr told him about the trip and all of its bad parts. She told him about freedom and all the things she knew.

He carried these new ideas in his head when he became president of the United States.

He told Zephyr's story to many government people and the Zephyr wind blew away their ideas about walls and locked doors.

Lady Bird's husband had to sign that law, and when he did he invited Zephyr to stand beside him. He gave her the pen he used and told her there was no one who deserved it more.

Today when you see a wall that has fallen or locked door open, and feel a breeze on your cheek.... It is Zephyr reminding you to let the wind carry you around obstacles, say no when you want to, and be sure to tell your story.

www.ingramcontent.com/pod-product-compliance
Lightning Source LLC
Chambersburg PA
CBHW042046290426
44109CB00001B/48